LOVE AND
RELATIONSHIPS

LOVE AND RELATIONSHIPS

Inspirations for
Meditation and Spiritual Growth

Edited by

EILEEN CAMPBELL

HarperSanFrancisco
A Division of HarperCollins*Publishers*

First published in Great Britain in 1992
as *A Lively Flame* by Aquarian/Thorsons,
an Imprint of HarperCollins*Publishers*

Library of Congress Cataloging-in-Publication Data:
Love and relationships: inspirations for meditation and
spiritual growth/edited by Eileen Campbell.
p. cm.
Originally published: A lively flame. London:
Aquarian/Thorsons, 1992
Includes bibliographical references.
ISBN 0-06-251324-9 (pbk. ; alk. paper)
1. Love—Quotations, maxims, etc. I. Campbell, Eileen.
PN6084.L6L58 1995
302.3—dc20 95-4230
CIP

ISBN 0-06-251324-9 (pbk)

95 96 97 98 99 UKA 10 9 8 7 6 5 4 3 2 1

This edition is printed on acid-free paper that meets the
American National Standards Institute Z39.48 Standard.

Love feels no burden, thinks nothing of trouble, attempts what is above its strength, pleads no excuse of impossibility... Though weary, it is not tired; though pressed, it is not straitened; though alarmed, it is not confounded; but like a lively flame and burning torch forces its way upwards and securely passes through all...

THOMAS À KEMPIS

INTRODUCTION

We all yearn for love and long to be in close relationship with others. Yet it is extraordinarily difficult
to achieve this. Whilst our relationships can be a
source of great fulfilment for us, they are also often
the cause of our greatest pain and sorrow.

Largely it is our understanding of love which is at
fault. A sense of oneness with what we love is what
we are seeking, but too often our expectations are
what lead us astray, and it is our perceptions which
need to change. Our love is too often conditional,
we do not accept people as they are, we do not love
enough.

To achieve love which is lasting and truly satisfying,

each of us must strive to cultivate love as a state of mind, and in giving love, we will receive it. Unconditional love knows no barriers and overcomes all difficulties. It is the only lesson we have to learn.

This anthology of quotations on love and relationships has been gathered from a wide variety of sources from both East and West. The quotations are loosely arranged in the following sequence: love and the nature of love, preparedness for love, falling in love, marriage and commitment, loss of love, love of God and universal love.

I hope that this anthology, which it has been a privilege to work on, may prove helpful at those times when the mind is far from peaceful.

What is wrong with our world is that
love is in short supply.

CHRISTOPHER BRYANT

The Eskimos had fifty-two names for snow
because it was important to them: there
ought to be as many for love.

MARGARET ATWOOD

One word frees us from the weight and pain
of life; that word is love.

SOPHOCLES

Oh, you who are trying to learn the marvel of Love through the copy book of reason, I'm very much afraid that you will never really see the point.

HAFIZ OF SHIRAZ

Love is the life of our heart. According to it, we desire, rejoice, hope and despair, fear, take heart, hate, avoid things, feel sad, grow angry and exult.

FRANCIS DE SALES

The main fact of life for me is love or its absence. Whether life is worth living depends on whether there is love in life.

R. D. LAING

The supreme happiness of life is the conviction that we are loved; loved for ourselves, or rather, loved in spite of ourselves.

VICTOR HUGO

The desire and pursuit
of the whole is called love.

PLATO

Love is an incurable disease.
No one who catches it wants to recover,
and all its victims refuse a cure.

IBN HAZIM

Affection as the essential principle of relatedness is of the greatest importance in all
relationships in the world. For the union of
heaven and earth is the origin of the whole
of nature. Among human beings likewise,
spontaneous affection is the all-inclusive
principle of union.

I CHING
THE MARRYING MAIDEN (HEXAGRAM 54)

Driven by the force of love the fragments of
the world seek each other that the world may
come into being.

TEILHARD DE CHARDIN

For as all true lovers

Know, love is perfect kindness,

Which is born – there is no doubt – from the
   heart and eyes.

The eyes make it blossom; the heart matures it:

Love, which is the fruit of Their very seed.

GUIRAUT DE BORNEILH

Since love is the most delicate and total act of a soul, it will reflect the state and nature of the soul. If the individual is not sensitive, how can his love be sentient? If he is not profound, how can his love be deep? As one is, so is his love.

JOSÉ ORTEGA Y GASSET

Love is a medicine for the sickness
of the world; a prescription often given,
too rarely taken.

KARL A. MENNINGER

Happiness and love are just a choice away.

LEO BUSCAGLIA

To fear love is to fear life.

BERTRAND RUSSELL

To love means never to be afraid of the windstorms of life: Should you shield the canyons from the windstorms you would never see the true beauty of their carvings.

ELISABETH KÜBLER-ROSS

You must love yourself before you love another. By accepting yourself and fully being what you are ... your simple presence can make others happy.

JANE ROBERTS

As long as we are looking outside ourselves for intimacy, we will never have it and we will never be able to share it. In order to be intimate with another person, we have to know who we are, what we feel, what we think, what our values are, what is important to us, and what we want. If we do not know these things about ourselves, we can never share them with another person.

ANNE WILSON SCHAEF

Love is the free exercise of choice. Two people love each other only when they are quite capable of living without each other but choose to live with each other.

M. SCOTT PECK

You want to be loved because you do not love; but the moment you love, it is finished, you are no longer inquiring whether or not somebody loves you.

J. KRISHNAMURTI

A Messenger called Love

'Why are you alone and so sad?' Love asked one day while He was on His journey upon Earth. He had been sent to Earth as a messenger, and He had been told to help people understand that they didn't have to feel lonely or unloved.

He said to the woman He had just met: 'I am Love and I have come to touch your life in a beautiful way. I can't stay long, for I have much to do, but maybe I can help you understand why you are lonely. I have met many people whose hearts are in isolation.'

The woman looked up at Love with tear-filled eyes and said, 'I am tired and exhausted from my search to love and be loved. I have experienced the beginnings of loving with others but all too soon loving departed, leaving wounds that have never fully healed. The times between feeling loved are so long that I am losing the will to try again. I have come to accept my fate and become a lonely old woman who lives on wishes and dreams.'

'But you don't have to accept that fate,' Love said with a gentle smile. 'I have encountered many souls as lonely as yourself, and the message I bring to all of you is simply this: If you learn to love yourself, and believe that you deserve the goodness life has to offer, then you will attract loving people to you. They will want to share who you are and to help you achieve your happiness.'

With these softly spoken words, Love turned to leave.

The woman, wide-eyed and excited, cried out, 'Don't leave me, Love! I have so many questions I would like to ask you! So much is still a mystery to me!'

Love replied as He began to vanish down the road, 'All the answers you seek are within you. Look there, for Love to replace your loneliness.'

WALTER RINDER

Most people see the problem of love as that
of being loved, rather than that of loving,
of one's capacity to love.

ERICH FROMM

Love knows no pain.

MEISTER ECKHART

We can never know love if we try to draw others to ourselves; nor can we find it by centering our love in them. For love is infinite; it is never ours to create. We can only channel it from its source in infinity to all whom we meet.

J. DONALD WALTERS

Love exists, regardless of our opinions about what it ought to be. No matter how many fabrications or how much selfishness we justify in the name of 'love', love still keeps its unchanging character. Its existence and its nature do not depend on my illusions, my opinions, or my counterfeits. Love is different from what my culture has led me to expect, different from what my ego wants, different from the sentimental froth and inflated ecstasies I've been taught to hope for; but love turns out to be real; it turns out to be what I am, rather than what my ego demands.

ROBERT A. JOHNSON

Everyone wants to be loved. But first we must make ourselves lovable. We must prepare ourselves to be loved. We do this by becoming ourselves loving, disciplined human beings. If we seek to be loved – if we expect to be loved – this cannot be accomplished; we will be dependent and grasping, not genuinely loving. But when we nurture ourselves and others without a primary concern of finding reward, then we will have become lovable, and the reward of being loved, which we have not sought, will find us. So it is with human love and so it is with God's love.

M. SCOTT PECK

To be loved for what one is, is the greatest exception. The great majority love in another only what they lend him, their own selves, their version of him.

J. W. von Goethe

Love from one being to another can only be
that two solitudes come nearer, recognize
and protect and comfort each other.

HAN SUYIN

And we are put on earth a little space
That we might learn to bear the beams
of love.

WILLIAM BLAKE

You know quite well deep within you, that
there is only a single magic, a single power, a
single salvation ... and that is called loving.

HERMANN HESSE

Love is ... not a result; it is a cause... People talk about love as though it were something you could give, like an armful of flowers... Love is a force in you that enables you to give other things... It is a power like money, or steam, or electricity. It is valueless unless you can give something else by *means* of it.

ANNE MORROW LINDBERGH

Therefore, when I say that 'I love,' it is not I who love, but in reality Love who acts through me. Love is not so much something I do as something that I am. Love is not a doing but a state of being – a relatedness, a connectedness to another mortal, an identification with her or him that simply flows within me and through me, independent of my intentions or my efforts.

ROBERT A. JOHNSON

Only in relationship can you know yourself,
not in abstraction, and certainly not
in isolation.

J. KRISHNAMURTI

Relationships are the temple of the
Holy Spirit.

———

A Course in Miracles

The greatest union is
that between man and woman,
corresponding as it does to the
turning of God toward the one created
in the Divine image, Allah's representative,
so that God might behold God.

IBN 'ARABI

Each lifetime
and each relationship within each lifetime
is an opportunity to experience love.
When you see each other
as the Divine and eternal beings that you are,
you will never cease to wonder and to glory
in the coming together. Do not be seduced
into seeing each other merely as the human
    shell.
Rather, see the soul, the consciousness within.

EMMANUEL

For love does not seek a joy that follows from its effect: its joy is in the effect itself, which is the good of the beloved. Consequently, if my love be pure I do not even have to seek for myself the satisfaction of loving. Love seeks one thing only: the good of the one loved.

THOMAS MERTON

Love does not consist in gazing at each other,
but in looking outward in the same direction.

Antoine de Saint-Exupéry

A relationship is not meant to be the joining at the hip of two emotional invalids. The purpose of a relationship is not for two incomplete people to become one, but rather for two complete people to join together for the greater glory of God.

MARIANNE WILLIAMSON

I define love thus: The will to extend one's self
for the purpose of nurturing one's own or
another's spiritual growth.

M. SCOTT PECK

Love is not primarily a relationship to a specific person; it is an *attitude, an orientation of character* which determines the relatedness of a person to the world as a whole, not towards one 'object' of love.

ERICH FROMM

When we genuinely love another person, it is a spontaneous act of being, an identification with the other person that causes us to affirm, value and honor him or her, to desire that person's happiness and well-being. In those rare moments when we are loving, rather than focused on our own egos, we stop asking what dreams this person is going to fulfill for us, what intense and extraordinary adventures he or she is going to provide.

ROBERT A. JOHNSON

Love is seldom spontaneous, instant, dynamic. It usually takes considerable time to create. It results from work, from thinking, from promoting equality, from being able to cope and adapt.

WILLIAM LEDERER

Love is a product of habit.

LUCRETIUS

Genuine love is volitional rather than emotional. The person who truly loves does so because of a decision to love. This person has made a commitment to be loving whether or not the loving feeling is present.

M. SCOTT PECK

Love means to commit oneself without guarantee, to give oneself completely in the hope that our love will produce love in the loved person. Love is an act of faith, and whoever is of little faith is of little love.

ERICH FROMM

To love at all is to be vulnerable.

C. S. LEWIS

Most of us in committed, stable relationships settle for predictability, comfort, and companionship because we fear exploring the mysteries that we embody together as man and woman, the exposure of our deepest selves. Yet in our fear of the unknown within us and between us we ignore and avoid the very gift that our commitment sets within our reach – true intimacy.

ROBIN NORWOOD

Love is letting go of fear.

GERALD JAMPOLSKY

There is no fear in love; but perfect love
casteth out fear: because fear hath torment.
He that feareth is not made perfect in love.

1 JOHN 4:18

When the heart is flooded with love there is no room in it for fear, for doubt, for hesitation. And it is this lack of fear that makes for the dance. When each partner loves so completely that he has forgotten to ask himself whether he is loved in return; when he only knows that he loves and is moving to music – then, and then only, are two people able to dance perfectly in time to the same rhythm.

ANNE MORROW LINDBERGH

Love means setting aside walls, fences, and unlocking doors, and saying YES... One can be in paradise by simply saying 'yes' to this moment.

E M M A N U E L

Perhaps love is the process of my leading you
gently back to yourself.

To love is to return to a home we never left,
to remember who we are.

SAM KEEN

Without warning,
As a whirlwind swoops upon an oak,
Love shakes my heart.

SAPPHO

Never, in sooth, does the lover seek without being sought by his beloved.

When the lightning of love has shot into this heart, know that there is love in *that* heart.

RŪMI

Love is an act of imagination. For some of us, it will be the great creative triumph of our lives. In its very nature as an act of the imagination lies the power for both good and ill, for it can indeed exploit the lovers' illusions or delusions, but alternately can lead the lover to transcending truths.

ETHEL SPECTOR PERSON

Falling in love is a creative act: we endow the beloved with all the magical powers of having generated this marvellous feeling in ourselves – and forget that it is we who have tapped our own creative force.

PENNY THORNTON

Listen to desire as you listen to the wind among the trees.

J. KRISHNAMURTI

Romantic love is not an aberration, it is the heady stuff that launches ships and makes the world go round. It is a powerful taste of the divine as we experience it in one another. It is also the necessary vision that allows one to be crazy and daring enough to make a commitment.

GERTRUDE MUELLER NELSON

We seek in romantic love to be possessed by our love, to soar to the heights, to find ultimate meaning and fulfillment in our beloved. We seek the feeling of wholeness.

If we ask where else we have looked for those things, there is a startling and troubling answer: religious experience. When we look for something greater than our egos, when we seek a vision of perfection, a sense of inner wholeness and unity, when we strive to rise above the smallness and partialness of personal life to something extraordinary and limitless, this is spiritual aspiration.

ROBERT A. JOHNSON

How do I love thee? Let me count the ways.
I love thee to the depth and breadth and height
My soul can reach, when feeling out of sight
For the ends of Being and ideal Grace…

ELIZABETH BARRETT BROWNING

Falling in love is actually a powerful experience of feeling the Universe move through you. The other person has become a channel for you, a catalyst that triggers you to open up to the love, beauty and compassion within.

SHAKTI GAWAIN

For two personalities to meet is like mixing two chemical substances: if there is any combination at all, both are transformed.

C. G. JUNG

At the core of our existence, we all experience the basic ache of feeling separate. We long to be united with someone or something outside of ourselves, so that we do not have to feel this ache so sharply. So when we finally find someone we feel close to, it may seem like a kind of salvation – no longer must we wander this lonely world all by ourselves. Yet in satisfying our urge to merge, it is all too easy to become submerged in a relationship, waking up one day to realize that we have lost something essential – ourself!

Relationships always involve this kind of fluctuation between bonding with another and

maintaining our integrity as individuals, yield-
ing to our partner and asserting ourselves,
reaching out and going deep within.

———

JOHN WELWOOD

The people we are in relationship with are always a mirror, reflecting our own beliefs, and simultaneously we are mirrors reflecting their beliefs. So relationship is one of the most powerful tools for growth ... if we look honestly at our relationships we can see so much about how we have created them.

SHAKTI GAWAIN

...the essential ingredients for relationship are affection and commitment... If it is romance that we seek, it is romance that we shall have, but not commitment and not relationship.

ROBERT A. JOHNSON

Love is blind, and lovers cannot see
The pretty follies that they themselves commit.

———

WILLIAM SHAKESPEARE
THE MERCHANT OF VENICE II.VI.

Of all the misconceptions about love the most powerful and pervasive is the belief that 'falling in love' is love or at least one of the manifestations of love.

M. SCOTT PECK

...to the extent that a relationship is founded on projection the element of human love is lacking. To be in love with someone we do not know as a person, but are attracted to because they reflect back to us the image of the god or goddess in our souls, is, in a sense, to be in love with oneself, not with the other person. In spite of the seeming beauty of the love fantasies we may have in this state of being in love, we can, in fact, be in a thoroughly selfish state of mind.

Real love begins only when one person comes to know another for who he or she really is as a human being, and begins to like and care for that human being.

...to be capable of real love means becoming mature, with realistic expectations of the other person. It means accepting responsibility for our own happiness or unhappiness, and neither expecting the other person to make us happy nor blaming that person for our bad moods and frustrations.

JOHN A. SANFORD

To love is to love the person.
It is not to love the good or the perfect things
to be found in that person.

GEORGETTE BUTCHER

Every relationship is in part composed of an objectification. It is also necessary to be able to observe the partner impartially and objectively. On the one hand, we experience in love a full identification with the other; on the other hand a cool objectivity should not be avoided. Without objectivity a relationship remains chaotic and dangerous.

ADOLF GUGGENBÜHL-CRAIG

Young people, who are beginners in every-thing, cannot yet know love, they have to learn it. With their whole being, with all their forces gathered close about their lonely, timid, upward-beating heart, they must learn to love. But learning-time is always a long, secluded time, and so loving, for a long while ahead and far on into life, is solitude, intensified and deepened loneness for him who loves. Love is at first not anything that means merging, giving over, and uniting with another (for what would a union be of something unclarified and individual) to ripen, to become something of himself, to become world, to become world for himself for another's sake; it is a great exacting claim upon him, something that chooses him out and calls him to vast things. Only in this sense as the task of working at themselves ('to hearken and to hammer day and night'), might young people use the love that is given them.

RAINER MARIA RILKE

Young love is a flame – very pretty – often very hot and fierce, but still only light and flickering. The love of the older and disciplined heart is as coals, deep-burning, unquenchable.

HENRY WARD BEECHER

The first steps to unselfish love is the recognition that our love may be deluded. We must first of all purify our love by renouncing the pleasure of loving as an end in itself. As long as pleasure is our end, we will be dishonest with ourselves and with those we love. We will not seek their good but our own pleasure.

THOMAS MERTON

When you are in love with someone, you do indeed see them as a divine being. Now, suppose that is what they truly are and that your eyes have by your beloved been opened. Through a tremendous outpouring of psychic energy in total devotion and worship for this other person, who is respectively god or goddess, you realize by total fusion and contact, the divine center in them. At once it bounces back to you and you discover your own.

ALAN WATTS

Set me as a seal upon your heart,
As a ring upon your arm;
For love is as strong as death...
Its flashes are flashes of fire,
A flame of the Eternal.

SONG OF SONGS VIII 6–7

Love is the power within us that affirms and values another human being as he or she is. Human love affirms that person who is actually there, rather than the ideal we would like him or her to be or the projection that flows from our minds. Love is the inner god who opens our blind eyes to the beauty, value, and quality of the other person. Love causes us to value that person as a total, individual self, and this means that we accept the negative side as well as the positive, the imperfections as well as the admirable qualities. When one truly loves the human being rather than the projection, one loves the shadow just as one loves the rest. One accepts the other person's totality.

ROBERT A. JOHNSON

For one human being to love another: that is
perhaps the most difficult of all our tasks, the
ultimate, the last test and proof, the work for
which all other work is but preparation.

RAINER MARIA RILKE

Let me not to the marriage of true minds
Admit impediments; love is not love
Which alters when it alteration finds,
Or bends with the remover to remove.
O, no, it is an ever-fixèd mark
That looks on tempests and is never shaken;
It is the star to every wand'ring bark,
Whose worth's unknown, although his height
    be taken.
Love's not Time's fool, though rosy lips and
    cheeks
Within his bending sickle's compass come;
Love alters not with his brief hours and weeks,
But bears it out even to the edge of doom.

If this be error and upon me proved,
I never writ, nor no man ever loved.

WILLIAM SHAKESPEARE
SONNET 116

Is not marriage an open question, when it is alleged, from the beginning of the world that such as are in the institution wish to get out, and such as are out wish to get in.

RALPH WALDO EMERSON

It does not much signify whom one marries,
as one is sure to find next morning that
it is someone else.

SAMUEL ROGERS

Marriage is sought and kept alive by a
deep yearning to know another and
be known by another.

JOHN PIERRAKOS

The notion of marrying for love is one of the most pathological experiments that a civilized society has ever imagined, namely, the basing of marriage, which is lasting, upon romance, which is a passing fancy.

M. DENIS DE ROUGEMONT

While I generally find that great myths are great precisely because they represent and embody great universal truths, the myth of romantic love is a dreadful lie. Perhaps it is a necessary lie in that it ensures the survival of the falling-in-love experience that traps us into marriage. But as a psychiatrist I weep in my heart almost daily for the ghastly confusion and suffering that this myth fosters. Millions of people waste a vast amount of energy desperately and futilely attempting to make the reality of their lives conform to the un-reality of the myth.

M. SCOTT PECK

If we did not look to marriage as the principal source of happiness, fewer marriages would end in tears.

———

ANTHONY STORR

Once the realization is accepted that even between the closest human beings infinite distances continue to exist, a wonderful living side by side can grow up, if they succeed in loving the distance between them, which makes it possible for each to see the other whole against a wide sky.

RAINER MARIA RILKE

An unholy relationship is based on differences,
where each one thinks
the other has what he has not...
A holy relationship starts from a different
   premise.
Each one has looked within and seen no lack.
Accepting his completion, he would extend it
by joining with another, whole as himself.

A COURSE IN MIRACLES

To some extent, each of us marries to make up for his own deficiencies. As a child, no one can stand alone against his family and the community, and in all but the most extreme circumstances, he is in no position to leave and to set up a life elsewhere. In order to survive as children, we have all had to exaggerate those aspects of ourselves that pleased those on whom we depended, and to disown those attitudes and behaviours that were unacceptable to them. As a result, to varying degrees, we have each grown into disproportionate configurations of what we could be as human beings. What we lack, we seek out and then struggle against in those whom we select as mates. We marry the other because he (or she) is different from us, and then we complain, 'Why can't he (or she) be more like me?'

SHELDON KOPP

An honorable human relationship – that is, one in which two people have the right to use the word 'love' – is a process, delicate, violent, often terrifying to both persons involved, a process of refining the truths they can tell each other. It is important to do this because it breaks down human self-delusion and isolation. It is important to do this because in so doing we do justice to our own complexity. It is important to do this because we can count on so few people to go that hard way with us.

ADRIENNE RICH

When love is strong, a man and woman can make their bed on a sword's blade. When love grows weak, a bed of 60 cubits is not large enough...

THE TALMUD

The couples whose marriage will certainly be endangered ... and possibly ruined, are those who have idolized Eros. They thought he had the power and truthfulness of a god. They expected that mere feeling would do for them, and permanently, all that was necessary. When this expectation is disappointed they throw the blame on Eros or, more usually, on their partners. In reality, however, Eros, having made his gigantic promise and shown you in glimpses what its performance would be like, has 'done his stuff'. He, like a godparent, makes the vows; it is we who must keep them. It is we who must labour to bring our daily life into even closer accordance with what the glimpses have revealed. We must do the works of Eros when Eros is not present.

C. S. LEWIS

Love is an ideal thing, marriage is a real thing;
a confusion of the real with the ideal never
goes unpunished.

J. W. VON GOETHE

With passion you want to possess. The conversion of passion into compassion is the whole problem of marriage.

JOSEPH CAMPBELL

Oh we've got to trust
one another again
in some essentials.

Not the narrow little
bargaining trust
that says: I'm for you
if you'll be for me.

But a bigger trust,
a trust of the sun
that does not bother about
    moth and rust,
and we see it shining
in one another.

Oh don't you trust me,
don't burden me
with your life and affairs: don't
    thrust me
into your cares.

But I think you may trust
the sun in me
that glows with just
as much glow as you see
in me, and no more.

 But if it warms
your heart's quick core
why then trust it, it forms
one faithfulness more.

And be, oh be
a sun to me,
not a weary insistent
personality –

but a sun that shines
and goes dark, but shines
again and entwines
with the sunshine in me
till we both of us
are more glorious
and more sunny.

D. H. LAWRENCE

Husband and wife are like the two equal parts of a soybean. If the two parts are put under the earth separately, they will not grow. The soybean will grow only when the parts are covered by the skin. Marriage is the skin which covers each of them and makes them one.

HARI DASS

Chains do not hold a marriage together. It is threads, hundreds of tiny threads which sew people together through the years. That is what makes a marriage last – more than passion or even sex.

SIMONE SIGNORET

A marriage only works if one opens himself to exactly that which he would never ask for otherwise. Only through rubbing oneself sore and losing oneself is one able to learn about oneself, God and the world.

ADOLF GUGGENBÜHL-CRAIG

The real relatedness between two people is experienced in the small tasks they do together: the quiet conversation when the day's upheavals are at rest, the soft word of understanding, the daily companionship, the encouragement offered in a difficult moment, the small gift when least expected, the spontaneous gesture of love.

ROBERT A. JOHNSON

The web of marriage is made by propinquity
in the day to day living, side by side, looking
outward and working in the same direction. It
is woven in space and in time of the substance
of life itself.

ANNE MORROW LINDBERGH

Love one another, but make not a bond of love;

Let it rather be a moving sea between the shore
of your souls.

Fill each other's cup but drink not from one
cup.

Give one another of your bread but eat not
from the same loaf;

Sing and dance together and be joyous,

but let each of you be alone,

Even as the strings of a lute are alone

though they quiver with the same music.

Give your hearts, but not into each other's
keeping.
For only the hand of Life can contain your
hearts.

And stand together yet not too near together:
For the pillars of the temple stand apart,
And the oak tree and the cypress grow
not in each other's shadow.

KHALIL GIBRAN

A marriage is like a long trip in a tiny row boat: if one passenger starts to rock the boat, the other has to steady it; otherwise, they will go to the bottom together.

DAVID REUBEN

Seldom or never does a marriage develop into an individual relationship smoothly and without crises. There is no birth of consciousness without pain.

C. G. JUNG

When two people fall in love they seek ... to possess the object of their desire and to be united with it and to hold on to it forever. In the confident illusion that this will happen a bride and a bridegroom may promise on their wedding day 'to love and to cherish till death us do part', but from the first day of the honeymoon they will discover that husbands and wives cannot possess each other. Then over the years they may learn, as they clash and quarrel and forgive, to respect each other as unique persons and to set each other free.

STEPHEN VERNEY

When people get married because they think it's a long-time love affair, they'll be divorced very soon, because all love affairs end in disappointment. But marriage is recognition of a spiritual identity. If we live a proper life, if our minds are on the right qualities in regarding the person of the opposite sex, we will find our proper male or female counterpart. But if we are distracted by certain sensuous interests, we'll marry the wrong person. By marrying the right person, we reconstruct the image of the incarnate God, and that's what marriage is.

JOSEPH CAMPBELL

Most married people must, to some extent,
renounce certain parts of their personalities;
they must sacrifice at the altar of marriage.

———

ADOLF GUGGENBÜHL-CRAIG

Love ceases to be a demon only when he
ceases to be a god.

M. DENIS DE ROUGEMONT

In the world of the unconscious, love is one of those great psychological forces that have the power to transform the ego. Love is the one power that awakens the ego to the existence of something outside itself, outside its plans, outside its empire, outside its security. Love relates the ego not only to the rest of the human race, but to the soul and to all the gods of the inner world.

ROBERT A. JOHNSON

A marriage is a commitment to that which you are. That person is literally your other half. And you and the other are one. A love affair isn't that. That is a relationship for pleasure, and when it gets to be unpleasurable, it's off. But a marriage is a life commitment, and a life commitment means the prime concern of your life. If marriage is not the prime concern, you're not married.

JOSEPH CAMPBELL

The central issue in marriage is not well-being or happiness; it is ... salvation. Marriage involves not only a man and a woman who happily love each other and raise offspring together, but rather two people who are trying to individuate, to find their 'soul's salvation'.

ADOLF GUGGENBÜHL-CRAIG

Turning a close relationship into a path of self-liberation necessitates a change in our perception of our partner. Instead of seeing him or her as someone who might satisfy our various imagined needs, we can begin to see them as someone who can help us fulfil our real quest – our quest for fulfilment. They are offering us the opportunity to notice our attachments and the ways in which they distort our perception and our thinking.

PETER RUSSELL

Marriage is not a static state between two unchanging people. Marriage is a psychological and spiritual journey that begins in the ecstasy of attraction, meanders through a rocky stretch of self-discovery, and culminates in the creation of an intimate, joyful, lifelong union.

HARVILLE HENDRIX

A life *allied* with mine, for the rest of our lives
– that is the miracle of marriage.

M. DENIS DE ROUGEMONT

Relationships are part of a vast plan for our enlightenment, the Holy Spirit's blueprint by which each individual soul is led to greater awareness and expanded love. Relationships are the Holy Spirit's laboratories in which he brings together people who have the maximal opportunity for mutual growth.

MARIANNE WILLIAMSON

Your heart is not living until it has experienced
pain… The pain of love breaks open the heart,
even if it is as hard as a rock.

HAZRAT INAYAT KHAN

When love beckons to you, follow him,
Though his ways are hard and steep.
And when his wings enfold you, yield to him,
Though the sword hidden among his pinions
    may wound you.
And when he speaks to you, believe in him,
Though his voice may shatter your dreams
as the north wind lays waste the garden.

For even as love crowns you so shall he crucify
    you.
Even as he is for your growth so is he for your
    pruning.

Even as he ascends to your height and caresses
    your tenderest branches that quiver in the
    sun,
So shall he descend to your roots and shake
    them in their clinging to the earth.

KHALIL GIBRAN

The reality is that all relationships inevitably will be dissolved and broken. The ultimate price exacted for commitment to other human beings rests in the inescapable fact that loss and pain will be experienced when they are gone, even to the point of jeopardizing one's physical health. It is a toll that no one can escape, and a price that everyone will be forced to pay repeatedly. Like the rise and fall of the ocean tides, disruptions of human relationships occur at regular intervals throughout life, and include the loss of parents, death of a mate, divorce, marital separation, death of family members, children leaving home, death of close friends, change of neighbourhoods, and loss of acquaintances by retirement from work. Infancy, adolescence, middle age, old age – all seasons of life involve human loss.

JAMES J. LYNCH

True love hurts. It always has to hurt. It must be painful to love someone, painful to leave them, you might have to die for them. When people marry they have to give up everything to love each other.

MOTHER TERESA

...I had to learn through my tortured years of longing that love could not be literalized; that love could not be found forever in the loved one as object. Love was not a possession I could own. There was, I learned, a dark death in the heart of love, a deep death through which I had to let myself descend before I could meet with love which was not power, before I could meet with love which was whole and holy.

LINDA SCHIERSE LEONARD

Where love reigns, there is no will to power; and where the will to power is paramount, love is lacking. The one is but the shadow of the other.

C. G. JUNG

How Love came in, I do not know,
Whether by th'eye, or eare, or no:
Or whether with the soule it came
(At first) infused with the same:
Whether in part 'tis here or there,
Or like the soule, whole every where:
This troubles me: but I as well
As any other, this can tell;
That when from hence she does depart
The out-let then is from the heart.

ROBERT HERRICK

Perfect love means to love the one through
whom one became unhappy.

SØREN KIERKEGAARD

From suffering I have learned this: that whoever is sore wounded by love will never be made whole unless she embraces the very same love which wounded her.

MECHTILD OF MAGDEBURG

Sometimes we may find that our partner continues to seek satisfaction in ways that we cannot live with. Nevertheless, when we decide to go our own way we still have a choice as to how we separate. We can separate with bad feelings, blaming the other's faults and unacceptable behaviour. Or we can separate with forgiveness, love and understanding.

PETER RUSSELL

Unless you can die when the dream is past –
Oh, never call it loving.

ELIZABETH BARRETT BROWNING

Love must be learned, and learned again and again; there is no end to it.

KATHERINE ANNE PORTER

Love is an act of endless forgiveness.

PETER USTINOV

...Genuine forgiveness is participation, reunion overcoming the powers of estrangement... We cannot love unless we have accepted forgiveness, and the deeper our experience of forgiveness is, the greater is our love.

PAUL TILLICH

Lift up your eyes
and look on one another in innocence
born of complete forgiveness of each other's
illusions.

A COURSE IN MIRACLES

To forgive is the highest, most beautiful form of love. In return, you will receive untold peace and happiness.

ROBERT MULLER

Let us be kinder to one another.

ALDOUS HUXLEY

The great tragedy of life is not that men
perish, but that they cease to love.

W. SOMERSET MAUGHAM

Love becomes the ultimate answer to the ultimate human question.

ARCHIBALD MACLEISH

Always search for your innermost nature
in those you are with
as rose oil imbibes from roses.

RŪMI

Love is not a problem, not an answer to a question. Love knows no question. It is the ground of all, and questions arise only insofar as we are divided, absent, estranged, alienated from that ground.

THOMAS MERTON

Where love is, what can be wanting?
Where it is not, what can possibly be
    profitable?

And in a sense love is everything. It is the key to life, and its influences are those that move the world. Live only in the thought of love for all and you will draw love to you from all.

RALPH WALDO TRINE

I give you a new commandment,
Love one another as I have loved you
that you too should love one another.

JOHN 13:34

The words of Jesus, 'Love one another as I
have loved you', must be not only a light to us
but a flame that consumes the self in us.

MOTHER TERESA

Do you love your Creator?
Then love your fellow beings first.

THE KORAN

The fountain stream of love rises in the love
for an individual, but spreads and falls
in universal love.

HAZRAT INAYAT KHAN

When there is no love pour in love,
and you shall draw out love.

ST JOHN OF THE CROSS

Love alone can unite living beings so as to complete and fulfill them ... for it alone joins them by what is deepest in themselves. All we need is to imagine our ability to love developing until it embraces the totality of men and of the earth.

TEILHARD DE CHARDIN

Love is a great thing, a good above all others,
which alone maketh every burden light.

THOMAS À KEMPIS

The day will come when, after harnessing the winds, the tides, and gravitation, we shall harness for God the energies of love. And on that day, for the second time in the history of the world, man will have discovered fire.

TEILHARD DE CHARDIN

Love conquers all things.

VIRGIL

There is no difficulty that enough love will not conquer; no disease that enough love will not heal; no door that enough love will not open... It makes no difference how deeply seated may be the trouble; how hopeless the outlook; how muddled the tangle; how great the mistake. A sufficient realization of love will dissolve it all. If only you could love enough you would be the happiest and most powerful being in the world.

EMMET FOX

Not to love is not to live, or it is to live a living death. The life that goes out in love to all is the life that is full, and rich, and continually expanding in beauty and in power.

RALPH WALDO TRINE

The only thing I know about love is that
love is all there is... Love can do all
but raise the dead.

EMILY DICKINSON

The more we forget ourselves in giving to others, the better we can understand what love really is. And the more we love as channels for God's love, the more we can understand that His is the one love in all the universe.

J. DONALD WALTERS

We must widen the circle of our love until it embraces the whole village; the village in turn must take into its fold the district; the district the province, and so on till the scope of our love encompasses the whole world.

GANDHI

Love is our only reason for living and the only purpose of life. We live for the sake of love, and we live seeking love... It is not surprising that we keep looking for love. All of us are nothing but vibrations of love. We are sustained by love, and in the end we merge back into love... This world is nothing but a school of love; our relationships with our husband or wife, with our children and parents, with our friends and relatives are the university in which we are meant to learn what love and devotion truly are.

Yet the love we experience through other people is just a shadow of the love of the inner Self. There is a sublime place inside us where love dwells... The love that pulses in the cave of the heart does not depend on anything outside. It does not expect anything. It is completely independent.

SWAMI MUKTANANDA

Falling in love with God can be very similar to falling in love with a human being.

LIONEL BLUE

But there is such a thing as genuine love, which is always considerate. Its distinguishing characteristic is, in fact, regard for personal dignity. Its effect is to stimulate self-respect in the other person. Its concern is to help the loved one become their true self. In a mysterious way such love finds its truest realization in its power to stimulate the other to attain their highest self-realization.

ROMANO GUARDINI

In a real conversation, a real lesson, a real embrace...in all these, what is essential takes place between them in a dimension which is accessible only to them both... If I and another 'happen' to one another, the sum does not exactly divide. There is a remainder somewhere, where the souls end and the world has not yet begun.

MARTIN BUBER

O God of Love, we pray Thee to give us love:

Love in our thinking, love in our speaking,

Love in our doing,

And love in the hidden places of our souls;

Love of our neighbours near and far;

Love of our friends old and new;

Love of those with whom we find it hard to
        bear,

And love of those who find it hard to bear with
        us;

Love of those with whom we work,

And love of those with whom we take our ease;

Love in joy, love in sorrow;

Love in life and love in death;

That so at length we may be worthy to dwell
        with Thee,

Who art eternal love.

WILLIAM TEMPLE

Let yourself be loved, O Beloved, in the One. And from this One move out into the world, carrying within you the great potent energies of life to green your world, to create planets, suns, stars, stones, waves, oceans, to create new forms of life and expression – whether a friendship, a feeling, or a new form of vocation.

RŪMI

Let the disciple cultivate love without measure toward all beings. Let him cultivate toward the whole world, above, below, around, a heart of love unstinted... For in all the world this state of heart is best.

BUDDHA

The aim of all spiritual practice is love.

SAI BABA

Do not waste time bothering whether you 'love' your neighbour; act as if you did. As soon as we do this we find one of the great secrets. When you are behaving as if you loved someone, you will presently come to love him.

C. S. LEWIS

May it be, O Lord, that I seek not so much to be consoled as to console, to be understood as to understand, to be loved as to love; because it is in giving oneself that one receives; it is in forgetting oneself that one is found.

St Francis of Assisi

And if you desire to have this intent [to reach God] summarized in one word, take but a little word of one syllable. And such a word is LOVE – and fasten this word to your heart so it may never go away no matter what befalls you. And if any thought presses on you to ask what you would have, answer with just this one word.

THE CLOUD OF UNKNOWING

The gift of love is the gift of the power and capacity to love, and therefore, to give love with full effect is also to receive it. So love can only be kept by being given away, and it can only be given perfectly when it is also received.

THOMAS MERTON

Only love can bring us peace. And the experience of love is a choice we make, a mental decision to see love as the only real purpose and value in any situation.

MARIANNE WILLIAMSON

Love is the Law of God. You live that you may learn to love. You love that you may learn to live. No other lesson is required of man.

MIKHAIL NAIMY

Spread love everywhere you go: first of all in your own home. Give love to your children, to your wife or husband, to a next door neighbour... Let no one ever come to you without leaving better and happier. Be the living expression of God's kindness; kindness in your face, kindness in your eyes, kindness in your smile, kindness in your warm greeting.

MOTHER TERESA

If you would learn the secret of right relations,
look only for the divine in people and things,
and leave all the rest to God.

J. ALLEN BOONE

There are no different categories of love. There isn't one kind of love between a mother and a child, and another between lovers, and another between friends. The love which is real is the love which lies at the heart of all relationships. That is the love of God and it doesn't change with form or circumstance.

MARIANNE WILLIAMSON

There is no path greater than love.
There is no law higher than love.
And there is no goal beyond love.
God and love are identical.

M E H E R B A B A

Divine love is perfect peace and joy...

WILLIAM LAW

God's pure sweet love is not confined
By creeds which segregate and raise a wall.
His love enfolds, embraces humankind.
No matter what ourselves or Him we call.
Then why not take Him at His word?
Why hold to creeds which tear apart?
But one thing matters, be it heard.
That brother love fill every heart.
There's but one thing the world has need to
    know,
There's but one balm for all our human woe:
There's but one way that leads to heaven
    above –
That way is human sympathy and love.

MAX HEINDELL

Love is not becoming, love is being.

In becoming, there is danger; there is fear.

In being, there is none of this at all.

You blossom, you burn, all for the sake of love.

What is there to live for, except one thing:

To be the love from which God has created us.

It is a gift from God,

Not given as something separate from Him,

But his very soul.

SWAMI CHIDVILASANANDA

Do not imagine that love to be true must be extraordinary. No, what we need in our love is the continuity to love the One we love. See how a lamp burns, by the continual consumption of the little drops of oil...

My children, what are these drops of oil in our lamps? They are the little things of everyday life: fidelity, punctuality, little words of kindness, just a little thought for others, those little acts of silence, of look and thought, of word and deed. These are the very drops of love that make our religious life burn with so much light.

MOTHER TERESA

Lover divine and perfect Comrade,
Waiting content, invisible yet, but certain,
Be thou my God.
Thou, thou, the Ideal Man,
Fair, able, beautiful, content and loving,
Complete in body and dilate in spirit,
Be thou my God.

WALT WHITMAN

Come down, O Love Divine,

Seek Thou this soul of mine,

    And visit it with Thine own ardour glowing;

O Comforter draw near,

Within my heart appear

    And kindle it, Thy holy flame bestowing.

BIANCO DA SIENA

Though I speak with the tongues of men and angels but have not love, I have become as a sounding brass or a clanging cymbal.

And though I have the gift of prophecy, and understand all mysteries and all knowledge, and though I have all faith so that I could remove mountains, but have not love, I am nothing.

And though I bestow all my goods to feed the poor, and though I give my body to be burned, but have not love, it profits me nothing.

Love suffers long and is kind; love does not envy; love does not parade itself, is not puffed up; does not behave rudely, does not seek its own, is not provoked, thinks no evil;

Does not rejoice in iniquity but rejoices in the truth. Bears all things, believes all things, hopes all things, endures all things.

Love never fails. But where there are prophecies, they will fail; where there are tongues, they will cease; where there is knowledge, it will vanish away.

For we know in part and we prophesy in part. But when that which is perfect has come, then that which is in part will be done away.

When I was a child, I spoke as a child, I understood as a child, I thought as a child; but when I became a man, I put away childish things.

For now we see through a glass darkly, but then face to face. Now I know in part, but then I shall know just as I am also known.

And now abide faith, hope, love these three; but the greatest of these is love.

1 CORINTHIANS 13

LOVE IS THE SECRET

Know thou of a certainty that Love is the secret of God's holy Dispensation, the manifestation of the All-Merciful, the fountain of spiritual outpourings. Love is heaven's kindly light, the Holy Spirit's eternal breath that vivifieth the human soul. Love is the cause of God's revelation unto man, the vital bond inherent, in accordance with the divine creation, in the realities of things. Love is the one means that ensureth true felicity both in this world and the next. Love is the light that guideth in darkness, the living link that uniteth God with man, that assureth the progress of every illumined soul. Love is the most great law that ruleth this mighty and heavenly cycle, the unique power that bindeth together the divers elements of this material world, the supreme magnetic force that directeth the movements of the spheres in the celestial realms. Love revealeth with unfailing and limitless power the mysteries latent in the universe. Love is the spirit of life unto the adorned body of mankind, the establisher of true civilisation in this mortal world and the shedder of imperishable glory upon every high aiming race and nation.

ABDU'L-BAHA

ACKNOWLEDGEMENTS AND FURTHER READING

The editor would like to thank the following authors and publishers for permission to reprint material from their works.

Andrews, Frank, *The Art and Practice of Loving: 144 ways to enrich your experience of love* (Rider, 1991).

Buscaglia, Leo F., *Living, Loving and Learning* (Ballantine, 1982).

Campbell, Joseph, *The Power of Myth* (Doubleday, 1988).

A Course in Miracles (Foundation for Inner Peace, 1975).

Fromm, Erich, *The Art of Loving* (Allen and Unwin, 1957).

Gawain, Shakti, and King, Laurel, *Living in the Light* (Eden Grove, 1988).

Gibran, Khalil, *The Prophet* (Heinemann, 1926).

Guggenbühl-Craig, Adolf, *Marriage Dead or Alive* (Spring Publications, 1977).

Hendrix, Harville, *Getting the Love You Want: A guide for couples* (Henry Holt, 1988).

Johnson, Robert A., *The Psychology of Romantic Love* (Arkana, 1987).

Khan, Hazrat Inayat, *Gayan, Vadan, Kirtan* (Sufi Order Publications, 1980).

Kopp, Sheldon, *If You Meet the Buddha on the Road, Kill Him!* (Science and Behavior Books, 1972).

Leonard, Linda Schierse, *On the Way to the Wedding: Transforming the love relationship* (Shambhala, 1987).

Lewis, C. S., *The Four Loves* (Fount, 1963).

Lindbergh, Anne Morrow, *Gifts from the Sea* (Pantheon Books, 1975).

McGuinness, Alan Loy, *The Romance Factor* (HarperSanFrancisco, 1982).

Merton, Thomas, *No Man is an Island* (Burns and Oates, 1955).

Nelson, Gertrude Mueller, *Here All Dwell Free: Stories to heal the wounded feminine* (Doubleday, 1991).

Peck, M. Scott, *The Road Less Travelled: A new psychology of love, traditional values and spiritual growth* (Hutchinson/Random Century, 1978).

Person, Ethel Spector, *Love and Fateful Encounters: The power of romantic passion* (Bloomsbury, 1989).

Peterson, Sylvia Ogden, *From Love That Hurts To Love That's Real: A recovery workbook* (Prentice Hall/Parkside, 1989).

Rilke, Rainer Maria, *Letters to a Young Poet* (Norton, 1934).

Rinder, Walter, *Forever Us* (Celestial Arts, 1981).

Rodegast, Pat, *Emmanuel's Book: A manual for living comfortably in the cosmos* (Bantam, 1987).

Russell, Peter, *A White Hole in Time* (The Aquarian Press, 1992).

Saint-Exupéry, Antoine de, *Wind, Sand and Stars* (Picador Books, 1987).

Sanford, John A., *The Invisible Partners* (Paulist Press, 1980).

Thornton, Penny, *Divine Encounters: A new kind of loving for a New Age of living* (The Aquarian Press, 1991).

Trine, Ralph Waldo, *In Tune With the Infinite* (The Aquarian Press, 1989).

Welwood, John, *Journey of the Heart: Intimate relationships and the path of love* (HarperCollins, 1990).

Williamson, Marianne, *A Return to Love: Reflections on the principles of 'A Course in Miracles'* (HarperCollins, 1992).